Motocross Racing

Jesse Young

Reading consultant:
John Manning, Professor of Reading
University of Minnesota

Capstone Press
M I N N E A P O L I S

Printed in the United States of America.

Capstone Press • 2440 Fernbrook Lane • Minneapolis, MN 55447

Editorial Director   John Coughlan
Managing Editor   John Martin
Copy Editor   Gil Chandler

Library of Congress Cataloging-in-Publication Data

Young, Jesse, 1941-
    Motocross racing / Jesse Young.
        p. cm. -- (Motorsports)
    Includes bibliographical references and index.
    ISBN 1-56065-228-4 : $13.35
    1. Motocross--Juvenile literature. [1. Motocross. 2. Motorcycle racing.]   I. Title.   II. Series.
    GV1060.12.Y68   1995
    796.7'56--dc20   94-26939
                                                                    CIP
                                                                    AC

ISBN: 1-56065-228-4

99 98 97 96   8 7 6 5 4 3 2

Table of Contents

Chapter 1
The Thrill of Motocross

Twenty dirt bikes rocket out of the **starting gate**. At the first turn, five are fighting for the lead. The racers ride over hills, dig into the turns, and soar 50 feet (15 meters) in the air. After one high jump, several hit the ground with a dull thump.

The five leaders round a **berm** when the leader loses control of his bike. He slides into one of the many haystacks you see lining the track. The riders behind him continue cautiously. The fallen rider sets his bike upright and rejoins the race.

He tries to catch the rest of the pack, but other riders pass him. He was the leader only seconds ago. Now he's battling to stay out of last place.

The racers dash around the track. Other riders lose control on dangerous **doubles** and tight corners. The pack leans into a turn as the drivers bump each other for a better position. At the finish, the front two bikes are just inches apart.

Speed, noise, excitement, and danger. This is the fast-paced world of motocross racing.

Chapter 2

The Rise of Dirt-Bike Racing

During the 1930s and 1940s, riders in the United States began to drive their Harley-Davidson and Indian street bikes on **off-road** courses. At the same time in Europe, off-road racers competed on their large European motorcycles.

But the Europeans found their bikes too clumsy for the narrow and bumpy off-road courses. These riders wanted bikes that were easier to handle. To meet the demand for a new kind of motorcycle, the Swedish company Husquavarna began to manufacture an off-road bike. It was lighter and easier to control.

Dirt bikes can take sharp turns and climb steep hills with ease.

The Sport of Motocross Grows

During the 1960s, dirt-bike racing quickly began to catch on in Europe and in the United States. As the sport grew, drivers began racing lighter and less-powerful motorcycles. By the early 1970s, riders everywhere were racing dirt bikes. People rushed to see the bumps, jumps, and turns of these races. Motocross was born.

Chapter 3
Motocross Racing

Although a Swedish company made the first off-road bikes, Japanese companies such as Honda, Kawasaki, Suzuki, and Yamaha dominate the business today.

The Bikes

Motocross bikes are made in different sizes. Cubic centimeters, or cc, is the scientific measurement for the size of a motorcycle's **cylinder**. The biggest and most powerful motorcycles have the largest cylinders. Because these motorcycles are more powerful than others, it wouldn't be fair to race them against smaller bikes. For this reason, motorcycles of the same size are grouped together in **classes**. Riders on one size of bike race only against the bikes in the same class.

Because motocross tracks are very rough, the bikes must have **shock absorbers**. When racers ride off large jumps, shock absorbers soften the landings. In the front, shock absorbers connect the wheel to the bike's **chassis**. The rear wheel is attached to a **swing arm**. The swing arm connects the wheel to the chassis.

Because of the rough tracks, the exhaust pipe on a motocross bike is placed high on the frame. There, it won't scrape the ground when the rider drives over bumps and loose rocks. The front fender is placed high above the wheel so it won't become clogged with mud.

The Track

Motocross tracks are between .5 and 2 miles (.8 and 3.2 kilometers) long. These tracks are built outdoors on natural **terrain**. Each track is

different. Riders have to deal with steep hills, tall jumps, and sometimes even trees.

Mounds of banked dirt, called berms, line the corners. Riders use these berms to take sharp turns. The slope of the berm helps keep the bike and the racer on the track.

A special challenge for the motocross racer is the "double." A double is a pair of jumps. If the racer goes fast enough, both hills can be cleared in one jump. If the racer does not clear the second jump, he's in for a painful fall.

Chapter 4
Supercross Racing

Supercross is a style of motocross always raced in stadiums. Track builders bring truckfuls of dirt into the stadium where they build the jumps, bumps, and berms.

Supercross has explosive starts and stops, fast crashes, and dangerous leaps. It also features the same motorcycles used in outdoor motocross.

Because of the speed and excitement, supercross attracts huge audiences. The large **purses** attract many racers. Add fireworks, lights, and music, and you have one of today's most successful sports: the supercross show.

The Track

Supercross tracks are different from motocross tracks. The supercross driver is challenged by more jumps and tighter turns. Supercross tracks also have short **straightaways**. But the racers do not have to tackle natural obstacles like steep hills and trees.

Because supercross tracks are built indoors, they are usually shorter than motocross tracks. On the fastest parts of the tracks, riders may reach speeds of 65 miles (105 kilometers) per hour.

Supercross Superstar

The superstar of supercross is Jeremy McGrath. When he was only 21 years old, he was the fastest supercross racer in the world. He had raced motocross since he was in high school.

McGrath began racing supercross in 1993. He won ten races that year–including the first one he entered!

Jeremy McGrath rockets toward the lead.

Chapter 5

Pacing the Race

S peed is important, but it is not the only thing in winning a motocross race. Motocross racing takes more **stamina** than any other sport except soccer. Each **moto** is about 30 to 45 minutes long. After one moto, the exhausted racer usually has only an hour to rest before the start of the next one. Riding too hard and too fast can blow out the motor and exhaust the rider. The racer must **pace** himself from start to finish in order to have any hope of winning.

Motocross racers often ask friends or family to hold up boards showing how far along the race is. These boards let the racer know where

he stands in the competition. He can then decide whether to save his energy or to go for the lead.

Motocross also requires exercise and training. The racers are always falling and getting back on their bikes. A professional racer once ran through a four-foot thick fence, got back up, and went right back into the race. Another broke his shoulder but was racing again just two weeks later.

Motocross racers must also take good care of their equipment. To handle a season of motocross, the bike's engine, suspension, and other important parts must stay in excellent condition. Professional riders employ mechanics, or "**wrenches**." They keep the motorcycles in top running order.

Sponsorship

Most professional racers work for motorcycle manufacturers. This way, they can test the bikes and offer suggestions for improving the company's motorcycles.

Chapter 6

How to Start Racing Motocross

In the United States, the American Motorcyclist Association (AMA) sanctions motocross racing. The AMA has 200,000 members. It was started in 1942 to protect the interests of motorcyclists.

Getting a Number

Once you sign up with an AMA district, you will receive a racing number. With a number,

Young riders get ready for the start of a moto.

you can race and win points at events the AMA sponsors.

You can call the AMA to find out about a district near you. Then you will be able to find information about schedules, racing numbers, and other questions you may have.

Moving Up

The AMA sponsors about 5,000 races a year. Most of these are for amateurs. About 500 of them are for professionals. Racers receive points for winning or placing high in official races. The number of points a racer has at the end of a season determines his **standing**.

The AMA records how many points you've won. If you're good enough, you will be able to advance to higher classes of competition. Each sponsored race offers awards for the winning riders.

Chapter 7
Safety

Motocross can be a fun sport. It can also be a dangerous one in which any rider can get hurt. Wearing protective clothing, and constant training, are two ways to keep the sport safe.

Know Your Skill Level

The most important thing is not to do more than you are capable of–no matter what you see the professional racers do. Smart riders ride safe.

Chapter 8

The Future of Motocross

Supercross and other arena events will continue to attract big audiences. Motorcycle manufacturers will keep improving their machines–especially if racers continue to tell them what works. And dirt-bike riders will enjoy the challenge of tackling rough and natural terrain.

Environmentalists will probably continue to protest motocross and its impact on nature. They will speak out against riders who damage the land. The AMA asks motorcyclists to quiet their machines around hikers and campers.

These people have a right to enjoy the outdoors, too.

Motocross may some day be as popular in the United States as it is in Europe. For young people, motocross has thrills and chills, lights and music. And you can watch it indoors or outdoors, like baseball. It's the ultimate mix of skill, stamina, and speed.

Glossary

berms–sloped mounds of dirt placed at the corners of motocross tracks

chassis–a sturdy frame which holds pieces of an engine together

class–a group of riders with motorcycles of the same size

cylinder–hollow part of an engine where gasoline is burned. The size of the tube determines the class of the motorcycle.

double–two jumps placed close together

environmentalist–one who wants to preserve and protect the natural world

moto–one of a series of motocross races

off-road–races which are not held on paved surfaces

pace–the rate of speed at which a person walks, runs, or races

purse–prize money awarded to the winner of a race

shock absorber–spring-like devices which cushion a bike's landing

stamina–the ability to withstand fatigue

standing–where a rider ranks among those he races against

starting gate–a device which drops to signal riders to begin racing

straightaway–a flat, straight surface on a motocross track

swing arm–a bar which connects the bike's rear wheel to the chassis

terrain–the features and shape of the land

wrenches–name given to the mechanics who work on motocross bikes

To Learn More

Baumann, Elwood D. *An Album of Motorcycles and Motorcycle Racing*. New York: Franklin Watts, 1982.

Carser, S.X. *Motocross Cycles*. Mankato, Minnesota: Capstone Press, 1992.

Jefferis, David. *Trail Bikes*. New York: Franklin Watts, 1984.

Yaw, John. *Motocross Motorcycle Racing*. Minneapolis: Lerner Publications, 1978.

Magazines

Dirt Bike Magazine
P.O. Box 958
Valencia, CA 91380-9058

Dirt Rider
Lee Cowie Motorsports
RR 1, Box 200D
Jonesburg, MO 63351

Some Useful Addresses

American Motorcyclist Association
P.O. Box 6114
Westerville, OH 43081
1-800-AMA-JOIN

Summers Racing Club
5769 Synder Lane
Petersburg, KY 41080

Index

Photo Credits:
All photographs courtesy of Jim Talkington, *Photography on Location.*

J
796.7   Young, Jesse
Y   Motocross racing

14.25

J
796.7   Young, Jesse
Y   Motocross racing

14.25

NOV 3 0 2001 A4066		
JAN 1 6 2003 A2135		